BLOG PLA

BLOG TITLE:

DOMAIN:

TARGET AUDIENCE:

NICHE OVERVIEW:

MAIN FOCUS:

PRIMARY KEYWORDS:

MAIN TRAFFIC SOURCES:

BLOG CONTROLS

ADMIN LOGIN:

AFFILIATE ACCOUNTS:

ADVERTISER ACCOUNTS:

HOSTING ACCOUNT LOGIN:

Important Contacts

PARTNERS:

OTHER:

SOCIAL MEDIA

TWITTER

FACEBOOK

INSTAGRAM

PINTEREST

OTHER

OTHER

OTHER

OTHER

BRAND CREATION

SLOGAN / TAGLINE:

_____

WRITING & CONTENT STYLE:

_____

_____

_____

NICHE SUMMARY:

_____

_____

_____

_____

6 WORDS TO DESCRIBE MY BLOG:

_____   _____

_____   _____

_____   _____

HOW MY BLOG PROVIDES VALUE:

_____

_____

_____

MISSION STATEMENT:

_____

_____

_____

_____

BLOG DESIGN

BLOG STYLE IDEAS

THEME USED:

BASE COLOR SCHEME:

PRIMARY FONTS USED:

LOGO / GRAPHIC DESIGNER:

DESIGN CHECKLIST:

- Verify responsive design
- Create 404 landing page
- Install contact form & opt in
- Create advertiser side widgets
- Test links in navigation menu
- Install Cookie Permission Plugin
- Install Privacy Agreement

PLUGIN CHECKLIST:

- Install SEO plugin
- Install WP Total Cache
- Install social sharing plugin
- Install WP Forms
- Install Google Analytics
- Install Backup Plugin
- Install Opt-in Plugin

AFFILIATE INCOME

ADVERTISER ACCOUNTS:

AFFILIATE ACCOUNTS:

JANUARY

TASKS, MARKETING, ENGAGEMENT & MONETIZATION

CONTENT IDEAS

PROMOTION IDEAS

TOP PRIORITIES

MONTHLY FOCUS

MONETIZATION IDEAS

MONTHLY GOALS

MAIN OBJECTIVE:

GOAL:

ACTION STEPS:

GOAL:

ACTION STEPS:

GOAL:

ACTION STEPS:

TRAFFIC STATS:

MAILING LIST SUBSCRIBERS:

CONTENT PLANNER

POST TITLE:

PUBLICATION DATE:

TARGETED KEYWORDS:

TO DO CHECKLIST:

- [ ] Research Topic
- [ ] Pinpoint Target Audience
- [ ] Choose target keywords
- [ ] Optimize for search engines
- [ ] Link to other blog post
- [ ] Create post images
- [ ] Proofread & Edit Post
- [ ] Schedule Post Date

SOCIAL SHARING: (circle all that apply)

TOPIC OUTLINE:

NOTES:

CONTENT PLANNER

CATEGORY:

RESOURCE LINKS:

GRAPHICS/IMAGES:

KEY POINTS:

SEO CHECKLIST:

- [ ] Primary keyword in post title
- [ ] Secondary keyword in sub-title
- [ ] Keyword in first paragraph
- [ ] Word count > 1000 words
- [ ] 1-2 Outbound Links
- [ ] Internal Link Structure
- [ ] Post URL includes keywords
- [ ] Meta description added
- [ ] Post includes images
- [ ] Post includes sub-headlines
- [ ] Social sharing enabled

NOTES:

POST PLANNER

WEEK OF: _____

TYPE: ARTICLE: ☐   TUTORIAL: ☐   REVIEW: ☐   GUEST POST: ☐

PUBLICATION DATE:

TITLE: _____

CATEGORY: _____

KEYWORDS: _____

NOTES: _____

_____

PUBLICATION DATE:

TITLE: _____

CATEGORY: _____

KEYWORDS: _____

NOTES: _____

_____

PUBLICATION DATE:

TITLE: _____

CATEGORY: _____

KEYWORDS: _____

NOTES: _____

_____

POST PLANNER

WEEK OF: _____

TYPE: ARTICLE: ☐   TUTORIAL: ☐   REVIEW: ☐   GUEST POST: ☐

PUBLICATION DATE:

TITLE: _____

CATEGORY: _____

KEYWORDS: _____

NOTES: _____

_____

LIST BUILDING PROGRESS:

 # SUBSCRIBERS: _____ ☐   **EMAILED THIS WEEK** ✉

SOCIAL MEDIA PROMO THIS WEEK:

☐ 🐦   ☐ f   ☐ 📌   ☐ 📷   ☐ ▶   in ☐ 8+

EXTERNAL LINKS:

INTERNAL LINKS:

PRODUCTS PROMOTED:

☐ Affiliate Disclaimer Included

MARKETING PLANNER

TOP TRAFFIC CHANNELS:

MARKETING TO DO LIST:

FREE ADVERTISING IDEAS:

PAID ADVERTISING IDEAS:

MARKETING PLANNER

PROMOTIONAL IDEAS:

MARKETING TO DO:

SOCIAL MEDIA GROWTH TRACKER:

	BEFORE:	AFTER:
f		
⃝		
🐦		
P		
▶		
OTHER:		

LIST BUILDING & ENGAGEMENT:

MAILING LIST
SUBSCRIBERS:

OF EMAILS SENT
TO SUBSCRIBERS:

OF NEW BLOG
POSTS THIS WEEK:

OF COMPLETED
GUEST POSTS:

NOTES:

GUEST BLOGGING

POST TITLE:

PUBLISH DATE:

CATEGORY:

MAIN TOPIC:

POST SUMMARY:

KEY POINTS:

☐ _____ ☐ _____

☐ _____ ☐ _____

INCLUDED LINKS:

_____

_____

SHARED ON:

FACEBOOK ☐   INSTAGRAM ☐

TWITTER ☐   PINTEREST ☐

☐   ☐

TAGS & KEYWORDS:

_____ ☐

_____ ☐

_____ ☐

 # OF COMMENTS: **# OF TRACKBACKS:**

NOTES:

FEBRUARY

TASKS, MARKETING, ENGAGEMENT & MONETIZATION

CONTENT IDEAS

PROMOTION IDEAS

TOP PRIORITIES

MONTHLY FOCUS

MONETIZATION IDEAS

MONTHLY GOALS

MAIN OBJECTIVE:

GOAL:

ACTION STEPS:

GOAL:

ACTION STEPS:

GOAL:

ACTION STEPS:

TRAFFIC STATS:

MAILING LIST SUBSCRIBERS:

CONTENT PLANNER

POST TITLE:

PUBLICATION DATE:

TARGETED KEYWORDS:

TO DO CHECKLIST:

- Research Topic
- Pinpoint Target Audience
- Choose target keywords
- Optimize for search engines
- Link to other blog post
- Create post images
- Proofread & Edit Post
- Schedule Post Date

SOCIAL SHARING: (circle all that apply)

TOPIC OUTLINE:

NOTES:

CONTENT PLANNER

CATEGORY:

RESOURCE LINKS:

GRAPHICS/IMAGES:

KEY POINTS:

SEO CHECKLIST:

- [ ] Primary keyword in post title
- [ ] Secondary keyword in sub-title
- [ ] Keyword in first paragraph
- [ ] Word count > 1000 words
- [ ] 1-2 Outbound Links
- [ ] Internal Link Structure
- [ ] Post URL includes keywords
- [ ] Meta description added
- [ ] Post includes images
- [ ] Post includes sub-headlines
- [ ] Social sharing enabled

NOTES:

POST PLANNER

WEEK OF: _____

TYPE: ARTICLE: ☐   TUTORIAL: ☐   REVIEW: ☐   GUEST POST: ☐

PUBLICATION DATE:

TITLE: _____

CATEGORY: _____

KEYWORDS: _____

NOTES: _____

_____

PUBLICATION DATE:

TITLE: _____

CATEGORY: _____

KEYWORDS: _____

NOTES: _____

_____

PUBLICATION DATE:

TITLE: _____

CATEGORY: _____

KEYWORDS: _____

NOTES: _____

_____

POST PLANNER

WEEK OF: _____

TYPE: ARTICLE: ☐ TUTORIAL: ☐ REVIEW: ☐ GUEST POST: ☐

PUBLICATION DATE:

TITLE: _____

CATEGORY: _____

KEYWORDS: _____

NOTES: _____

_____

LIST BUILDING PROGRESS:

 # SUBSCRIBERS: _____ ☐ **EMAILED THIS WEEK** ✉

SOCIAL MEDIA PROMO THIS WEEK:

☐ 🐦 ☐ f ☐ 𝓟 ☐ 📷 ☐ ▶ ☐ in ☐ g+

EXTERNAL LINKS:

PRODUCTS PROMOTED:

INTERNAL LINKS:

☐ Affiliate Disclaimer Included

POST PLANNER

WEEK OF: _____

TYPE: ARTICLE: ☐   TUTORIAL: ☐   REVIEW: ☐   GUEST POST: ☐

PUBLICATION DATE:

TITLE: _____

CATEGORY: _____

KEYWORDS: _____

NOTES: _____

_____

LIST BUILDING PROGRESS:

 # SUBSCRIBERS: _____ ☐   **EMAILED THIS WEEK** ✉

SOCIAL MEDIA PROMO THIS WEEK:

☐ 🐦   ☐ f   ☐ 𝓟   ☐ 📷   ☐ ▶   ☐ in   ☐ g+

EXTERNAL LINKS:

PRODUCTS PROMOTED:

INTERNAL LINKS:

☐ Affiliate Disclaimer Included

MARKETING PLANNER

TOP TRAFFIC CHANNELS:

MARKETING TO DO LIST:

FREE ADVERTISING IDEAS:

PAID ADVERTISING IDEAS:

MARKETING PLANNER

PROMOTIONAL STRATEGIES TO MAXIMIZE EXPOSURE

PROMOTIONAL IDEAS:

MARKETING TO DO:

SOCIAL MEDIA GROWTH TRACKER:

	BEFORE:	AFTER:
f		
⬛		
🐦		
🅿		
▶		
OTHER:		

LIST BUILDING & ENGAGEMENT:

MAILING LIST SUBSCRIBERS:

 # OF EMAILS SENT TO SUBSCRIBERS:

 # OF NEW BLOG POSTS THIS WEEK:

 # OF COMPLETED GUEST POSTS:

NOTES:

GUEST BLOGGING

POST TITLE:

PUBLISH DATE: CATEGORY:

MAIN TOPIC:

POST SUMMARY:

KEY POINTS:

- ☐ _____   ☐ _____
- ☐ _____   ☐ _____

INCLUDED LINKS:

_____

_____

SHARED ON:

FACEBOOK	☐	INSTAGRAM	☐
TWITTER	☐	PINTEREST	☐
	☐		☐

TAGS & KEYWORDS:

_____ ☐

_____ ☐

_____ ☐

# OF COMMENTS:	# OF TRACKBACKS:

NOTES:

MARCH

TASKS, MARKETING, ENGAGEMENT & MONETIZATION

CONTENT IDEAS

PROMOTION IDEAS

TOP PRIORITIES

MONTHLY FOCUS

MONETIZATION IDEAS

MONTHLY GOALS

MAIN OBJECTIVE:

GOAL:

ACTION STEPS:

GOAL:

ACTION STEPS:

GOAL:

ACTION STEPS:

TRAFFIC STATS:

MAILING LIST SUBSCRIBERS:

CONTENT PLANNER

POST TITLE:

_____

PUBLICATION DATE:

_____

TARGETED KEYWORDS:

_____

_____

_____

TO DO CHECKLIST:

- Research Topic
- Pinpoint Target Audience
- Choose target keywords
- Optimize for search engines
- Link to other blog post
- Create post images
- Proofread & Edit Post
- Schedule Post Date

SOCIAL SHARING: (circle all that apply)

TOPIC OUTLINE:

_____

_____

_____

_____

_____

_____

NOTES:

CONTENT PLANNER

CATEGORY:

RESOURCE LINKS:

GRAPHICS/IMAGES:

KEY POINTS:

SEO CHECKLIST:

- [ ] Primary keyword in post title
- [ ] Secondary keyword in sub-title
- [ ] Keyword in first paragraph
- [ ] Word count > 1000 words
- [ ] 1-2 Outbound Links
- [ ] Internal Link Structure
- [ ] Post URL includes keywords
- [ ] Meta description added
- [ ] Post includes images
- [ ] Post includes sub-headlines
- [ ] Social sharing enabled

NOTES:

POST PLANNER

WEEK OF: _____

TYPE: ARTICLE: ☐   TUTORIAL: ☐   REVIEW: ☐   GUEST POST: ☐

PUBLICATION DATE:

TITLE: _____

CATEGORY: _____

KEYWORDS: _____

NOTES: _____

PUBLICATION DATE:

TITLE: _____

CATEGORY: _____

KEYWORDS: _____

NOTES: _____

PUBLICATION DATE:

TITLE: _____

CATEGORY: _____

KEYWORDS: _____

NOTES: _____

POST PLANNER

WEEK OF: _____

TYPE: ARTICLE: ☐ TUTORIAL: ☐ REVIEW: ☐ GUEST POST: ☐

PUBLICATION DATE:

TITLE: _____

CATEGORY: _____

KEYWORDS: _____

NOTES: _____

_____

LIST BUILDING PROGRESS:

SUBSCRIBERS: _____ ☐ EMAILED THIS WEEK ✉

SOCIAL MEDIA PROMO THIS WEEK:

☐ 🐦 ☐ f ☐ 𝓟 ☐ 📷 ☐ ▶ ☐ in ☐ 8+

EXTERNAL LINKS:

PRODUCTS PROMOTED:

INTERNAL LINKS:

☐ Affiliate Disclaimer Included

POST PLANNER

WEEK OF: _____

TYPE: ARTICLE: ☐   TUTORIAL: ☐   REVIEW: ☐   GUEST POST: ☐

PUBLICATION DATE:

TITLE: _____

CATEGORY: _____

KEYWORDS: _____

NOTES: _____

_____

LIST BUILDING PROGRESS:

 # SUBSCRIBERS: _____ ☐ **EMAILED THIS WEEK** ✉

SOCIAL MEDIA PROMO THIS WEEK:

☐ 🐦   ☐ f   ☐ 𝒫   ☐ 📷   ☐ ▶   ☐ in   ☐ G+

EXTERNAL LINKS:

INTERNAL LINKS:

PRODUCTS PROMOTED:

☐ Affiliate Disclaimer Included

MARKETING PLANNER

TOP TRAFFIC CHANNELS:

MARKETING TO DO LIST:

FREE ADVERTISING IDEAS:

PAID ADVERTISING IDEAS:

MARKETING PLANNER

PROMOTIONAL STRATEGIES TO MAXIMIZE EXPOSURE

PROMOTIONAL IDEAS:

MARKETING TO DO:

SOCIAL MEDIA GROWTH TRACKER:

	BEFORE:	AFTER:
f		
(Instagram)		
(Twitter)		
(Pinterest)		
(YouTube)		
OTHER:		

LIST BUILDING & ENGAGEMENT:

MAILING LIST SUBSCRIBERS:

 # OF EMAILS SENT TO SUBSCRIBERS:

 # OF NEW BLOG POSTS THIS WEEK:

 # OF COMPLETED GUEST POSTS:

NOTES:

GUEST BLOGGING

POST TITLE:

PUBLISH DATE: CATEGORY:

MAIN TOPIC:

POST SUMMARY:

KEY POINTS:

INCLUDED LINKS:

SHARED ON:

FACEBOOK   INSTAGRAM

TWITTER   PINTEREST

TAGS & KEYWORDS:

 # OF COMMENTS: **# OF TRACKBACKS:**

NOTES:

APRIL

TASKS, MARKETING, ENGAGEMENT & MONETIZATION

CONTENT IDEAS

PROMOTION IDEAS

TOP PRIORITIES

MONTHLY FOCUS

MONETIZATION IDEAS

MONTHLY GOALS

MAIN OBJECTIVE:

GOAL:

ACTION STEPS:

GOAL:

ACTION STEPS:

GOAL:

ACTION STEPS:

TRAFFIC STATS:

MAILING LIST SUBSCRIBERS:

CONTENT PLANNER

POST TITLE:

_____

TARGETED KEYWORDS:

_____

_____

_____

SOCIAL SHARING: (circle all that apply)

TOPIC OUTLINE:

_____

_____

_____

_____

_____

_____

PUBLICATION DATE:

_____

TO DO CHECKLIST:

- [ ] Research Topic
- [ ] Pinpoint Target Audience
- [ ] Choose target keywords
- [ ] Optimize for search engines
- [ ] Link to other blog post
- [ ] Create post images
- [ ] Proofread & Edit Post
- [ ] Schedule Post Date

NOTES:

CONTENT PLANNER

CATEGORY:

RESOURCE LINKS:

GRAPHICS/IMAGES:

KEY POINTS:

SEO CHECKLIST:

- [ ] Primary keyword in post title
- [ ] Secondary keyword in sub-title
- [ ] Keyword in first paragraph
- [ ] Word count > 1000 words
- [ ] 1-2 Outbound Links
- [ ] Internal Link Structure
- [ ] Post URL includes keywords
- [ ] Meta description added
- [ ] Post includes images
- [ ] Post includes sub-headlines
- [ ] Social sharing enabled

NOTES:

POST PLANNER

WEEK OF: _____

TYPE: ARTICLE: ☐ TUTORIAL: ☐ REVIEW: ☐ GUEST POST: ☐

PUBLICATION DATE:

TITLE: _____

CATEGORY: _____

KEYWORDS: _____

NOTES: _____

_____

PUBLICATION DATE:

TITLE: _____

CATEGORY: _____

KEYWORDS: _____

NOTES: _____

_____

PUBLICATION DATE:

TITLE: _____

CATEGORY: _____

KEYWORDS: _____

NOTES: _____

_____

POST PLANNER

WEEK OF: _____

TYPE: ARTICLE: ☐ TUTORIAL: ☐ REVIEW: ☐ GUEST POST: ☐

PUBLICATION DATE:

TITLE: _____

CATEGORY: _____

KEYWORDS: _____

NOTES: _____

_____

LIST BUILDING PROGRESS:

 # SUBSCRIBERS: _____ ☐ **EMAILED THIS WEEK** ✉

SOCIAL MEDIA PROMO THIS WEEK:

☐ 🐦 ☐ f ☐ 🅿 ☐ 📷 ☐ ▶ ☐ in ☐ 8+

EXTERNAL LINKS:

PRODUCTS PROMOTED:

INTERNAL LINKS:

☐ Affiliate Disclaimer Included

POST PLANNER

WEEK OF: _____

TYPE: ARTICLE: ☐   TUTORIAL: ☐   REVIEW: ☐   GUEST POST: ☐

PUBLICATION DATE:

TITLE: _____

CATEGORY: _____

KEYWORDS: _____

NOTES: _____

_____

LIST BUILDING PROGRESS:

 # SUBSCRIBERS: _____   ☐   **EMAILED THIS WEEK** ✉

SOCIAL MEDIA PROMO THIS WEEK:

☐ 🐦   ☐ f   ☐ 𝕻   ☐ 📷   ☐ ▶   in ☐ G+

EXTERNAL LINKS:

PRODUCTS PROMOTED:

INTERNAL LINKS:

☐ Affiliate Disclaimer Included

MARKETING PLANNER

TOP TRAFFIC CHANNELS:

MARKETING TO DO LIST:

FREE ADVERTISING IDEAS:

PAID ADVERTISING IDEAS:

MARKETING PLANNER

PROMOTIONAL IDEAS:

MARKETING TO DO:

SOCIAL MEDIA GROWTH TRACKER:

	BEFORE:	AFTER:
f		
Instagram		
Twitter		
Pinterest		
YouTube		
OTHER:		

LIST BUILDING & ENGAGEMENT:

MAILING LIST
SUBSCRIBERS:

OF EMAILS SENT
TO SUBSCRIBERS:

OF NEW BLOG
POSTS THIS WEEK:

OF COMPLETED
GUEST POSTS:

NOTES:

GUEST BLOGGING

POST TITLE:

PUBLISH DATE:	CATEGORY:

MAIN TOPIC:

POST SUMMARY:

KEY POINTS:

☐ _____   ☐ _____

☐ _____   ☐ _____

INCLUDED LINKS:	SHARED ON:	FACEBOOK ☐	INSTAGRAM ☐
_____		TWITTER ☐	PINTEREST ☐
_____		☐	☐

TAGS & KEYWORDS:	# OF COMMENTS:	# OF TRACKBACKS:
_____ ☐		
_____ ☐	**NOTES:**	
_____ ☐		

MAY

TASKS, MARKETING, ENGAGEMENT & MONETIZATION

CONTENT IDEAS

PROMOTION IDEAS

TOP PRIORITIES

MONTHLY FOCUS

MONETIZATION IDEAS

MONTHLY GOALS

MAIN OBJECTIVE:

GOAL:

ACTION STEPS:

GOAL:

ACTION STEPS:

GOAL:

ACTION STEPS:

TRAFFIC STATS:

MAILING LIST SUBSCRIBERS:

CONTENT PLANNER

POST TITLE:

PUBLICATION DATE:

TARGETED KEYWORDS:

TO DO CHECKLIST:

- Research Topic
- Pinpoint Target Audience
- Choose target keywords
- Optimize for search engines
- Link to other blog post
- Create post images
- Proofread & Edit Post
- Schedule Post Date

SOCIAL SHARING: (circle all that apply)

TOPIC OUTLINE:

NOTES:

CONTENT PLANNER

CATEGORY:

RESOURCE LINKS:

GRAPHICS/IMAGES:

KEY POINTS:

SEO CHECKLIST:

- [ ] Primary keyword in post title
- [ ] Secondary keyword in sub-title
- [ ] Keyword in first paragraph
- [ ] Word count > 1000 words
- [ ] 1-2 Outbound Links
- [ ] Internal Link Structure
- [ ] Post URL includes keywords
- [ ] Meta description added
- [ ] Post includes images
- [ ] Post includes sub-headlines
- [ ] Social sharing enabled

NOTES:

POST PLANNER

WEEK OF: _____

TYPE: ARTICLE: ☐ TUTORIAL: ☐ REVIEW: ☐ GUEST POST: ☐

PUBLICATION DATE:

TITLE: _____

CATEGORY: _____

KEYWORDS: _____

NOTES: _____

_____

PUBLICATION DATE:

TITLE: _____

CATEGORY: _____

KEYWORDS: _____

NOTES: _____

_____

PUBLICATION DATE:

TITLE: _____

CATEGORY: _____

KEYWORDS: _____

NOTES: _____

_____

POST PLANNER

WEEK OF: _____

TYPE: ARTICLE: ☐ TUTORIAL: ☐ REVIEW: ☐ GUEST POST: ☐

PUBLICATION DATE:

TITLE: _____

CATEGORY: _____

KEYWORDS: _____

NOTES: _____

_____

LIST BUILDING PROGRESS:

SUBSCRIBERS: _____ ☐ EMAILED THIS WEEK ✉

SOCIAL MEDIA PROMO THIS WEEK:

☐ 🐦 ☐ f ☐ 🅿 ☐ 📷 ☐ ▶ ☐ in ☐ g+

EXTERNAL LINKS:

PRODUCTS PROMOTED:

INTERNAL LINKS:

☐ Affiliate Disclaimer Included

POST PLANNER

WEEK OF: _____

TYPE: ARTICLE: ☐ TUTORIAL: ☐ REVIEW: ☐ GUEST POST: ☐

PUBLICATION DATE:

TITLE: _____

CATEGORY: _____

KEYWORDS: _____

NOTES: _____

_____

LIST BUILDING PROGRESS:

 # SUBSCRIBERS: _____ ☐ **EMAILED THIS WEEK** ✉

SOCIAL MEDIA PROMO THIS WEEK:

☐ 🐦 ☐ f ☐ 𝓟 ☐ 📷 ☐ ▶ ☐ in ☐ g+

EXTERNAL LINKS:

PRODUCTS PROMOTED:

INTERNAL LINKS:

☐ Affiliate Disclaimer Included

MARKETING PLANNER

TOP TRAFFIC CHANNELS:

MARKETING TO DO LIST:

FREE ADVERTISING IDEAS:

PAID ADVERTISING IDEAS:

MARKETING PLANNER

PROMOTIONAL STRATEGIES TO MAXIMIZE EXPOSURE

PROMOTIONAL IDEAS:

MARKETING TO DO:

SOCIAL MEDIA GROWTH TRACKER:

	BEFORE:	AFTER:
f		
Instagram		
Twitter		
Pinterest		
YouTube		
OTHER:		

LIST BUILDING & ENGAGEMENT:

MAILING LIST
SUBSCRIBERS:

OF EMAILS SENT
TO SUBSCRIBERS:

OF NEW BLOG
POSTS THIS WEEK:

OF COMPLETED
GUEST POSTS:

NOTES:

GUEST BLOGGING

POST TITLE:

PUBLISH DATE:

CATEGORY:

MAIN TOPIC:

POST SUMMARY:

KEY POINTS:

☐ _____   ☐ _____

☐ _____   ☐ _____

INCLUDED LINKS:

_____

_____

SHARED ON:

FACEBOOK ☐   INSTAGRAM ☐

TWITTER ☐   PINTEREST ☐

☐   ☐

TAGS & KEYWORDS:

_____ ☐

_____ ☐

_____ ☐

OF COMMENTS: # OF TRACKBACKS:

NOTES:

JUNE

TASKS, MARKETING, ENGAGEMENT & MONETIZATION

CONTENT IDEAS

PROMOTION IDEAS

TOP PRIORITIES

MONTHLY FOCUS

MONETIZATION IDEAS

MONTHLY GOALS

MAIN OBJECTIVE:

GOAL:

ACTION STEPS:

GOAL:

ACTION STEPS:

GOAL:

ACTION STEPS:

TRAFFIC STATS:

MAILING LIST SUBSCRIBERS:

CONTENT PLANNER

POST TITLE:

PUBLICATION DATE:

TARGETED KEYWORDS:

TO DO CHECKLIST:

Research Topic

Pinpoint Target Audience

Choose target keywords

Optimize for search engines

Link to other blog post

Create post images

Proofread & Edit Post

Schedule Post Date

SOCIAL SHARING: (circle all that apply)

TOPIC OUTLINE:

NOTES:

CONTENT PLANNER

CATEGORY:

RESOURCE LINKS:

GRAPHICS/IMAGES:

KEY POINTS:

SEO CHECKLIST:

- [ ] Primary keyword in post title
- [ ] Secondary keyword in sub-title
- [ ] Keyword in first paragraph
- [ ] Word count > 1000 words
- [ ] 1-2 Outbound Links
- [ ] Internal Link Structure
- [ ] Post URL includes keywords
- [ ] Meta description added
- [ ] Post includes images
- [ ] Post includes sub-headlines
- [ ] Social sharing enabled

NOTES:

POST PLANNER

WEEK OF: _____

TYPE: ARTICLE: ☐ TUTORIAL: ☐ REVIEW: ☐ GUEST POST: ☐

PUBLICATION DATE:

TITLE: _____

CATEGORY: _____

KEYWORDS: _____

NOTES: _____

_____

PUBLICATION DATE:

TITLE: _____

CATEGORY: _____

KEYWORDS: _____

NOTES: _____

_____

PUBLICATION DATE:

TITLE: _____

CATEGORY: _____

KEYWORDS: _____

NOTES: _____

_____

POST PLANNER

WEEK OF: _____

TYPE: ARTICLE: ☐   TUTORIAL: ☐   REVIEW: ☐   GUEST POST: ☐

PUBLICATION DATE:

TITLE: _____

CATEGORY: _____

KEYWORDS: _____

NOTES: _____

_____

LIST BUILDING PROGRESS:

 # SUBSCRIBERS: _____ ☐   **EMAILED THIS WEEK** ✉

SOCIAL MEDIA PROMO THIS WEEK:

☐ 🐦   ☐ f   ☐ 𝓟   ☐ 📷   ☐ ▶   ☐ in   ☐ g+

EXTERNAL LINKS:

INTERNAL LINKS:

PRODUCTS PROMOTED:

☐ Affiliate Disclaimer Included

POST PLANNER

WEEK OF: _____

TYPE: ARTICLE: ☐   TUTORIAL: ☐   REVIEW: ☐   GUEST POST: ☐

PUBLICATION DATE:

TITLE: _____

CATEGORY: _____

KEYWORDS: _____

NOTES: _____

_____

LIST BUILDING PROGRESS:

 # SUBSCRIBERS: _____   ☐   **EMAILED THIS WEEK** ✉

SOCIAL MEDIA PROMO THIS WEEK:

☐ 🐦   ☐ f   ☐ 𝓟   ☐ 📷   ☐ ▶   in   ☐ g+

EXTERNAL LINKS:

PRODUCTS PROMOTED:

INTERNAL LINKS:

☐ Affiliate Disclaimer Included

MARKETING PLANNER

TOP TRAFFIC CHANNELS:

MARKETING TO DO LIST:

FREE ADVERTISING IDEAS:

PAID ADVERTISING IDEAS:

MARKETING PLANNER

PROMOTIONAL STRATEGIES TO MAXIMIZE EXPOSURE

PROMOTIONAL IDEAS:

MARKETING TO DO:

SOCIAL MEDIA GROWTH TRACKER:

	BEFORE:	AFTER:
f		
Instagram		
Twitter		
Pinterest		
YouTube		
OTHER:		

LIST BUILDING & ENGAGEMENT:

MAILING LIST SUBSCRIBERS:

OF EMAILS SENT TO SUBSCRIBERS:

OF NEW BLOG POSTS THIS WEEK:

OF COMPLETED GUEST POSTS:

NOTES:

GUEST BLOGGING

POST TITLE:

PUBLISH DATE:	CATEGORY:

MAIN TOPIC:

POST SUMMARY:

KEY POINTS:

- ☐ _____
- ☐ _____

☐ _____
☐ _____

INCLUDED LINKS:

_____
_____

SHARED ON:

FACEBOOK ☐	INSTAGRAM ☐
TWITTER ☐	PINTEREST ☐
☐	☐

TAGS & KEYWORDS:

_____ ☐
_____ ☐
_____ ☐

# OF COMMENTS:	# OF TRACKBACKS:

NOTES:

JULY

TASKS, MARKETING, ENGAGEMENT & MONETIZATION

CONTENT IDEAS

PROMOTION IDEAS

TOP PRIORITIES

MONTHLY FOCUS

MONETIZATION IDEAS

MONTHLY GOALS

MAIN OBJECTIVE:

GOAL:

ACTION STEPS:

GOAL:

ACTION STEPS:

GOAL:

ACTION STEPS:

TRAFFIC STATS:

MAILING LIST SUBSCRIBERS:

CONTENT PLANNER

POST TITLE:

PUBLICATION DATE:

TARGETED KEYWORDS:

TO DO CHECKLIST:

- Research Topic
- Pinpoint Target Audience
- Choose target keywords
- Optimize for search engines
- Link to other blog post
- Create post images
- Proofread & Edit Post
- Schedule Post Date

SOCIAL SHARING: (circle all that apply)

TOPIC OUTLINE:

NOTES:

CONTENT PLANNER

CATEGORY:

RESOURCE LINKS:

GRAPHICS/IMAGES:

KEY POINTS:

SEO CHECKLIST:

- [ ] Primary keyword in post title
- [ ] Secondary keyword in sub-title
- [ ] Keyword in first paragraph
- [ ] Word count > 1000 words
- [ ] 1-2 Outbound Links
- [ ] Internal Link Structure
- [ ] Post URL includes keywords
- [ ] Meta description added
- [ ] Post includes images
- [ ] Post includes sub-headlines
- [ ] Social sharing enabled

NOTES:

POST PLANNER

WEEK OF: _____

TYPE: ARTICLE: ☐ TUTORIAL: ☐ REVIEW: ☐ GUEST POST: ☐

PUBLICATION DATE:

TITLE: _____

CATEGORY: _____

KEYWORDS: _____

NOTES: _____

_____

PUBLICATION DATE:

TITLE: _____

CATEGORY: _____

KEYWORDS: _____

NOTES: _____

_____

PUBLICATION DATE:

TITLE: _____

CATEGORY: _____

KEYWORDS: _____

NOTES: _____

_____

POST PLANNER

WEEK OF: _____

TYPE: ARTICLE: ☐   TUTORIAL: ☐   REVIEW: ☐   GUEST POST: ☐

PUBLICATION DATE:

TITLE: _____

CATEGORY: _____

KEYWORDS: _____

NOTES: _____

_____

LIST BUILDING PROGRESS:

SUBSCRIBERS: _____ ☐ **EMAILED THIS WEEK** ✉

SOCIAL MEDIA PROMO THIS WEEK:

☐ 🐦   ☐ f   ☐ 𝓟   ☐ 📷   ☐ ▶   ☐ in   ☐ g+

EXTERNAL LINKS:

PRODUCTS PROMOTED:

INTERNAL LINKS:

☐ Affiliate Disclaimer Included

MARKETING PLANNER

TOP TRAFFIC CHANNELS:

MARKETING TO DO LIST:

FREE ADVERTISING IDEAS:

PAID ADVERTISING IDEAS:

MARKETING PLANNER

PROMOTIONAL IDEAS:

MARKETING TO DO:

SOCIAL MEDIA GROWTH TRACKER:

BEFORE: **AFTER:**

f

instagram

twitter

pinterest

youtube

OTHER:

LIST BUILDING & ENGAGEMENT:

MAILING LIST SUBSCRIBERS:

 # OF EMAILS SENT TO SUBSCRIBERS:

 # OF NEW BLOG POSTS THIS WEEK:

 # OF COMPLETED GUEST POSTS:

NOTES:

GUEST BLOGGING

POST TITLE:

PUBLISH DATE:	CATEGORY:

MAIN TOPIC:

POST SUMMARY:

KEY POINTS:

- ☐ _____
- ☐ _____
- ☐ _____
- ☐ _____

INCLUDED LINKS:

SHARED ON:

FACEBOOK ☐	INSTAGRAM ☐
TWITTER ☐	PINTEREST ☐
☐	☐

TAGS & KEYWORDS:

- _____ ☐
- _____ ☐
- _____ ☐

# OF COMMENTS:	# OF TRACKBACKS:

NOTES:

AUGUST

TASKS, MARKETING, ENGAGEMENT & MONETIZATION

CONTENT IDEAS

PROMOTION IDEAS

TOP PRIORITIES

MONTHLY FOCUS

MONETIZATION IDEAS

MONTHLY GOALS

MAIN OBJECTIVE:

GOAL:

ACTION STEPS:

GOAL:

ACTION STEPS:

GOAL:

ACTION STEPS:

TRAFFIC STATS:

MAILING LIST SUBSCRIBERS:

CONTENT PLANNER

POST TITLE:

PUBLICATION DATE:

TARGETED KEYWORDS:

TO DO CHECKLIST:

- Research Topic
- Pinpoint Target Audience
- Choose target keywords
- Optimize for search engines
- Link to other blog post
- Create post images
- Proofread & Edit Post
- Schedule Post Date

SOCIAL SHARING: (circle all that apply)

TOPIC OUTLINE:

NOTES:

CONTENT PLANNER

CATEGORY:

RESOURCE LINKS:

GRAPHICS/IMAGES:

KEY POINTS:

SEO CHECKLIST:

- [ ] Primary keyword in post title
- [ ] Secondary keyword in sub-title
- [ ] Keyword in first paragraph
- [ ] Word count > 1000 words
- [ ] 1-2 Outbound Links
- [ ] Internal Link Structure
- [ ] Post URL includes keywords
- [ ] Meta description added
- [ ] Post includes images
- [ ] Post includes sub-headlines
- [ ] Social sharing enabled

NOTES:

POST PLANNER

WEEK OF: _____

TYPE: ARTICLE: ☐ TUTORIAL: ☐ REVIEW: ☐ GUEST POST: ☐

PUBLICATION DATE:

TITLE: _____

CATEGORY: _____

KEYWORDS: _____

NOTES: _____

_____

PUBLICATION DATE:

TITLE: _____

CATEGORY: _____

KEYWORDS: _____

NOTES: _____

_____

PUBLICATION DATE:

TITLE: _____

CATEGORY: _____

KEYWORDS: _____

NOTES: _____

_____

POST PLANNER

WEEK OF: _____

TYPE: ARTICLE: ☐   TUTORIAL: ☐   REVIEW: ☐   GUEST POST: ☐

PUBLICATION DATE:

TITLE: _____

CATEGORY: _____

KEYWORDS: _____

NOTES: _____

_____

LIST BUILDING PROGRESS:

 # SUBSCRIBERS: _____ ☐ **EMAILED THIS WEEK** ✉

SOCIAL MEDIA PROMO THIS WEEK:

☐ 🐦 ☐ f ☐ 𝓟 ☐ 📷 ☐ ▶ ☐ in ☐ g+

EXTERNAL LINKS:

INTERNAL LINKS:

PRODUCTS PROMOTED:

☐ Affiliate Disclaimer Included

MARKETING PLANNER

TOP TRAFFIC CHANNELS:

MARKETING TO DO LIST:

FREE ADVERTISING IDEAS:

PAID ADVERTISING IDEAS:

MARKETING PLANNER

PROMOTIONAL STRATEGIES TO MAXIMIZE EXPOSURE

PROMOTIONAL IDEAS:

MARKETING TO DO:

SOCIAL MEDIA GROWTH TRACKER:

BEFORE: AFTER:

f

Instagram

Twitter

Pinterest

YouTube

OTHER:

LIST BUILDING & ENGAGEMENT:

MAILING LIST
SUBSCRIBERS:

OF EMAILS SENT
TO SUBSCRIBERS:

OF NEW BLOG
POSTS THIS WEEK:

OF COMPLETED
GUEST POSTS:

NOTES:

GUEST BLOGGING

POST TITLE:

PUBLISH DATE: CATEGORY:

MAIN TOPIC:

POST SUMMARY:

KEY POINTS:

☐ _____   ☐ _____
☐ _____   ☐ _____

INCLUDED LINKS:

_____

_____

SHARED ON:

FACEBOOK ☐   INSTAGRAM ☐

TWITTER ☐   PINTEREST ☐

☐   ☐

TAGS & KEYWORDS:

_____ ☐

_____ ☐

_____ ☐

 # OF COMMENTS: **# OF TRACKBACKS:**

NOTES:

SEPTEMBER

TASKS, MARKETING, ENGAGEMENT & MONETIZATION

CONTENT IDEAS

PROMOTION IDEAS

TOP PRIORITIES

MONTHLY FOCUS

MONETIZATION IDEAS

MONTHLY GOALS

MAIN OBJECTIVE:

GOAL:

ACTION STEPS:

GOAL:

ACTION STEPS:

GOAL:

ACTION STEPS:

TRAFFIC STATS:

MAILING LIST SUBSCRIBERS:

CONTENT PLANNER

POST TITLE:

_____

TARGETED KEYWORDS:

_____

_____

_____

SOCIAL SHARING: (circle all that apply)

TOPIC OUTLINE:

_____

_____

_____

_____

_____

_____

_____

PUBLICATION DATE:

_____

TO DO CHECKLIST:

- Research Topic
- Pinpoint Target Audience
- Choose target keywords
- Optimize for search engines
- Link to other blog post
- Create post images
- Proofread & Edit Post
- Schedule Post Date

NOTES:

CONTENT PLANNER

CATEGORY:

RESOURCE LINKS:

GRAPHICS/IMAGES:

KEY POINTS:

SEO CHECKLIST:

- [ ] Primary keyword in post title
- [ ] Secondary keyword in sub-title
- [ ] Keyword in first paragraph
- [ ] Word count > 1000 words
- [ ] 1-2 Outbound Links
- [ ] Internal Link Structure
- [ ] Post URL includes keywords
- [ ] Meta description added
- [ ] Post includes images
- [ ] Post includes sub-headlines
- [ ] Social sharing enabled

NOTES:

POST PLANNER

WEEK OF: _____

TYPE: ARTICLE: ☐   TUTORIAL: ☐   REVIEW: ☐   GUEST POST: ☐

PUBLICATION DATE:

TITLE: _____

CATEGORY: _____

KEYWORDS: _____

NOTES: _____

_____

PUBLICATION DATE:

TITLE: _____

CATEGORY: _____

KEYWORDS: _____

NOTES: _____

_____

PUBLICATION DATE:

TITLE: _____

CATEGORY: _____

KEYWORDS: _____

NOTES: _____

_____

POST PLANNER

WEEK OF: _____

TYPE: ARTICLE: ☐   TUTORIAL: ☐   REVIEW: ☐   GUEST POST: ☐

PUBLICATION DATE:

TITLE: _____

CATEGORY: _____

KEYWORDS: _____

NOTES: _____

_____

LIST BUILDING PROGRESS:

 # SUBSCRIBERS: _____   ☐   **EMAILED THIS WEEK** ✉

SOCIAL MEDIA PROMO THIS WEEK:

☐ 🐦   ☐ f   ☐ 𝒫   ☐ 📷   ☐ ▶   ☐ in   ☐ g+

EXTERNAL LINKS:

INTERNAL LINKS:

PRODUCTS PROMOTED:

☐ Affiliate Disclaimer Included

MARKETING PLANNER

TOP TRAFFIC CHANNELS:

MARKETING TO DO LIST:

FREE ADVERTISING IDEAS:

PAID ADVERTISING IDEAS:

MARKETING PLANNER

PROMOTIONAL STRATEGIES TO MAXIMIZE EXPOSURE

PROMOTIONAL IDEAS:

MARKETING TO DO:

SOCIAL MEDIA GROWTH TRACKER:

	BEFORE:	AFTER:
f		
Instagram		
Twitter		
Pinterest		
YouTube		
OTHER:		

LIST BUILDING & ENGAGEMENT:

MAILING LIST SUBSCRIBERS:

 # OF EMAILS SENT TO SUBSCRIBERS:

 # OF NEW BLOG POSTS THIS WEEK:

 # OF COMPLETED GUEST POSTS:

NOTES:

GUEST BLOGGING

POST TITLE:

PUBLISH DATE:	CATEGORY:

MAIN TOPIC:

POST SUMMARY:

KEY POINTS:

- ☐ _____
- ☐ _____
- ☐ _____
- ☐ _____

INCLUDED LINKS:

_____

_____

SHARED ON:

FACEBOOK	☐	INSTAGRAM	☐
TWITTER	☐	PINTEREST	☐
	☐		☐

TAGS & KEYWORDS:

_____ ☐

_____ ☐

_____ ☐

# OF COMMENTS:	# OF TRACKBACKS:

NOTES:

OCTOBER

TASKS, MARKETING, ENGAGEMENT & MONETIZATION

CONTENT IDEAS

PROMOTION IDEAS

TOP PRIORITIES

MONTHLY FOCUS

MONETIZATION IDEAS

MONTHLY GOALS

MAIN OBJECTIVE:

GOAL:

ACTION STEPS:

GOAL:

ACTION STEPS:

GOAL:

ACTION STEPS:

TRAFFIC STATS:

MAILING LIST SUBSCRIBERS:

CONTENT PLANNER

POST TITLE:

PUBLICATION DATE:

TARGETED KEYWORDS:

TO DO CHECKLIST:

Research Topic

Pinpoint Target Audience

Choose target keywords

Optimize for search engines

Link to other blog post

Create post images

Proofread & Edit Post

Schedule Post Date

SOCIAL SHARING: (circle all that apply)

TOPIC OUTLINE:

NOTES:

CONTENT PLANNER

CATEGORY:

_____

RESOURCE LINKS:

_____

_____

_____

GRAPHICS/IMAGES:

_____

_____

KEY POINTS:

_____

_____

_____

_____

_____

_____

_____

SEO CHECKLIST:

- [ ] Primary keyword in post title
- [ ] Secondary keyword in sub-title
- [ ] Keyword in first paragraph
- [ ] Word count > 1000 words
- [ ] 1-2 Outbound Links
- [ ] Internal Link Structure
- [ ] Post URL includes keywords
- [ ] Meta description added
- [ ] Post includes images
- [ ] Post includes sub-headlines
- [ ] Social sharing enabled

NOTES:

POST PLANNER

WEEK OF: _____

TYPE: ARTICLE: ☐　TUTORIAL: ☐　REVIEW: ☐　GUEST POST: ☐

PUBLICATION DATE:

TITLE: _____

CATEGORY: _____

KEYWORDS: _____

NOTES: _____

_____

PUBLICATION DATE:

TITLE: _____

CATEGORY: _____

KEYWORDS: _____

NOTES: _____

_____

PUBLICATION DATE:

TITLE: _____

CATEGORY: _____

KEYWORDS: _____

NOTES: _____

_____

POST PLANNER

WEEK OF: _____

TYPE: ARTICLE: ☐ TUTORIAL: ☐ REVIEW: ☐ GUEST POST: ☐

PUBLICATION DATE:

TITLE: _____

CATEGORY: _____

KEYWORDS: _____

NOTES: _____

_____

LIST BUILDING PROGRESS:

 # SUBSCRIBERS: _____ ☐ **EMAILED THIS WEEK** ✉

SOCIAL MEDIA PROMO THIS WEEK:

☐ 🐦 ☐ f ☐ 🅿 ☐ 📷 ☐ ▶ ☐ in ☐ g+

EXTERNAL LINKS:

INTERNAL LINKS:

PRODUCTS PROMOTED:

☐ Affiliate Disclaimer Included

MARKETING PLANNER

TOP TRAFFIC CHANNELS:

MARKETING TO DO LIST:

FREE ADVERTISING IDEAS:

PAID ADVERTISING IDEAS:

MARKETING PLANNER

PROMOTIONAL STRATEGIES TO MAXIMIZE EXPOSURE

PROMOTIONAL IDEAS:

MARKETING TO DO:

SOCIAL MEDIA GROWTH TRACKER:

	BEFORE:	AFTER:
f		
Instagram		
Twitter		
Pinterest		
YouTube		
OTHER:		

LIST BUILDING & ENGAGEMENT:

MAILING LIST SUBSCRIBERS:

OF EMAILS SENT TO SUBSCRIBERS:

OF NEW BLOG POSTS THIS WEEK:

OF COMPLETED GUEST POSTS:

NOTES:

GUEST BLOGGING

POST TITLE:

PUBLISH DATE:

CATEGORY:

MAIN TOPIC:

POST SUMMARY:

KEY POINTS:

☐ _____   ☐ _____

☐ _____   ☐ _____

INCLUDED LINKS:

_____

_____

FACEBOOK ☐   INSTAGRAM ☐

TWITTER ☐   PINTEREST ☐

☐   ☐

TAGS & KEYWORDS:

_____ ☐

_____ ☐

_____ ☐

 # OF COMMENTS: **# OF TRACKBACKS:**

NOTES:

NOVEMBER

TASKS, MARKETING, ENGAGEMENT & MONETIZATION

CONTENT IDEAS

PROMOTION IDEAS

TOP PRIORITIES

MONTHLY FOCUS

MONETIZATION IDEAS

MONTHLY GOALS

MAIN OBJECTIVE:

GOAL:

ACTION STEPS:

GOAL:

ACTION STEPS:

GOAL:

ACTION STEPS:

TRAFFIC STATS:

MAILING LIST SUBSCRIBERS:

CONTENT PLANNER

POST TITLE:

PUBLICATION DATE:

TARGETED KEYWORDS:

TO DO CHECKLIST:

- Research Topic
- Pinpoint Target Audience
- Choose target keywords
- Optimize for search engines
- Link to other blog post
- Create post images
- Proofread & Edit Post
- Schedule Post Date

SOCIAL SHARING: (circle all that apply)

TOPIC OUTLINE:

NOTES:

CONTENT PLANNER

CATEGORY:

RESOURCE LINKS:

GRAPHICS/IMAGES:

KEY POINTS:

SEO CHECKLIST:

- [ ] Primary keyword in post title
- [ ] Secondary keyword in sub-title
- [ ] Keyword in first paragraph
- [ ] Word count > 1000 words
- [ ] 1-2 Outbound Links
- [ ] Internal Link Structure
- [ ] Post URL includes keywords
- [ ] Meta description added
- [ ] Post includes images
- [ ] Post includes sub-headlines
- [ ] Social sharing enabled

NOTES:

POST PLANNER

WEEK OF: _____

TYPE: ARTICLE: ☐   TUTORIAL: ☐   REVIEW: ☐   GUEST POST: ☐

PUBLICATION DATE:

TITLE: _____

CATEGORY: _____

KEYWORDS: _____

NOTES: _____

_____

PUBLICATION DATE:

TITLE: _____

CATEGORY: _____

KEYWORDS: _____

NOTES: _____

_____

PUBLICATION DATE:

TITLE: _____

CATEGORY: _____

KEYWORDS: _____

NOTES: _____

_____

POST PLANNER

WEEK OF: _____

TYPE: ARTICLE: ☐ TUTORIAL: ☐ REVIEW: ☐ GUEST POST: ☐

PUBLICATION DATE:

TITLE: _____

CATEGORY: _____

KEYWORDS: _____

NOTES: _____

_____

LIST BUILDING PROGRESS:

 # SUBSCRIBERS: _____ ☐ **EMAILED THIS WEEK** ✉

SOCIAL MEDIA PROMO THIS WEEK:

☐ 🐦 ☐ f ☐ 𝓟 ☐ 📷 ☐ ▶ ☐ in ☐ g+

EXTERNAL LINKS:

PRODUCTS PROMOTED:

INTERNAL LINKS:

☐ Affiliate Disclaimer Included

POST PLANNER

WEEK OF: _____

TYPE: ARTICLE: ☐ TUTORIAL: ☐ REVIEW: ☐ GUEST POST: ☐

PUBLICATION DATE:

TITLE: _____

CATEGORY: _____

KEYWORDS: _____

NOTES: _____

_____

LIST BUILDING PROGRESS:

 # SUBSCRIBERS: _____ ☐ **EMAILED THIS WEEK** ✉

SOCIAL MEDIA PROMO THIS WEEK:

☐ 🐦 ☐ f ☐ 𝓟 ☐ 📷 ☐ ▶ ☐ in ☐ g+

EXTERNAL LINKS:

INTERNAL LINKS:

PRODUCTS PROMOTED:

☐ Affiliate Disclaimer Included

MARKETING PLANNER

TOP TRAFFIC CHANNELS:

MARKETING TO DO LIST:

FREE ADVERTISING IDEAS:

PAID ADVERTISING IDEAS:

MARKETING PLANNER

PROMOTIONAL STRATEGIES TO MAXIMIZE EXPOSURE

PROMOTIONAL IDEAS:

MARKETING TO DO:

SOCIAL MEDIA GROWTH TRACKER:

	BEFORE:	AFTER:
f		
(Instagram)		
(Twitter)		
(Pinterest)		
(YouTube)		
OTHER:		

LIST BUILDING & ENGAGEMENT:

MAILING LIST SUBSCRIBERS:

OF EMAILS SENT TO SUBSCRIBERS:

OF NEW BLOG POSTS THIS WEEK:

OF COMPLETED GUEST POSTS:

NOTES:

GUEST BLOGGING

POST TITLE:

PUBLISH DATE:

CATEGORY:

MAIN TOPIC:

POST SUMMARY:

KEY POINTS:

INCLUDED LINKS:

SHARED ON:

FACEBOOK

INSTAGRAM

TWITTER

PINTEREST

TAGS & KEYWORDS:

 # OF COMMENTS:

 # OF TRACKBACKS:

NOTES:

DECEMBER

TASKS, MARKETING, ENGAGEMENT & MONETIZATION

CONTENT IDEAS

PROMOTION IDEAS

TOP PRIORITIES

MONTHLY FOCUS

MONETIZATION IDEAS

MONTHLY GOALS

MAIN OBJECTIVE:

GOAL:

ACTION STEPS:

GOAL:

ACTION STEPS:

GOAL:

ACTION STEPS:

TRAFFIC STATS:

MAILING LIST SUBSCRIBERS:

CONTENT PLANNER

POST TITLE:

PUBLICATION DATE:

TARGETED KEYWORDS:

TO DO CHECKLIST:

- [ ] Research Topic
- [ ] Pinpoint Target Audience
- [ ] Choose target keywords
- [ ] Optimize for search engines
- [ ] Link to other blog post
- [ ] Create post images
- [ ] Proofread & Edit Post
- [ ] Schedule Post Date

SOCIAL SHARING: (circle all that apply)

TOPIC OUTLINE:

NOTES:

CONTENT PLANNER

CATEGORY:

RESOURCE LINKS:

GRAPHICS/IMAGES:

KEY POINTS:

SEO CHECKLIST:

- [ ] Primary keyword in post title
- [ ] Secondary keyword in sub-title
- [ ] Keyword in first paragraph
- [ ] Word count > 1000 words
- [ ] 1-2 Outbound Links
- [ ] Internal Link Structure
- [ ] Post URL includes keywords
- [ ] Meta description added
- [ ] Post includes images
- [ ] Post includes sub-headlines
- [ ] Social sharing enabled

NOTES:

POST PLANNER

WEEK OF: _____

TYPE: ARTICLE: ☐   TUTORIAL: ☐   REVIEW: ☐   GUEST POST: ☐

PUBLICATION DATE:

TITLE: _____

CATEGORY: _____

KEYWORDS: _____

NOTES: _____

_____

PUBLICATION DATE:

TITLE: _____

CATEGORY: _____

KEYWORDS: _____

NOTES: _____

_____

PUBLICATION DATE:

TITLE: _____

CATEGORY: _____

KEYWORDS: _____

NOTES: _____

_____

POST PLANNER

WEEK OF: _____

TYPE: ARTICLE: ☐   TUTORIAL: ☐   REVIEW: ☐   GUEST POST: ☐

PUBLICATION DATE:

TITLE: _____

CATEGORY: _____

KEYWORDS: _____

NOTES: _____

_____

LIST BUILDING PROGRESS:

 # SUBSCRIBERS: _____ ☐ **EMAILED THIS WEEK** ✉

SOCIAL MEDIA PROMO THIS WEEK:

☐ 🐦   ☐ f   ☐ 🅿   ☐ 📷   ☐ ▶   ☐ in   ☐ 8+

EXTERNAL LINKS:

INTERNAL LINKS:

PRODUCTS PROMOTED:

☐ Affiliate Disclaimer Included

MARKETING PLANNER

TOP TRAFFIC CHANNELS:

MARKETING TO DO LIST:

FREE ADVERTISING IDEAS:

PAID ADVERTISING IDEAS:

MARKETING PLANNER

PROMOTIONAL IDEAS:

MARKETING TO DO:

SOCIAL MEDIA GROWTH TRACKER:

BEFORE: AFTER:

OTHER:

LIST BUILDING & ENGAGEMENT:

MAILING LIST
SUBSCRIBERS:

OF EMAILS SENT
TO SUBSCRIBERS:

OF NEW BLOG
POSTS THIS WEEK:

OF COMPLETED
GUEST POSTS:

NOTES:

GUEST BLOGGING

POST TITLE:

PUBLISH DATE:	CATEGORY:

MAIN TOPIC:

POST SUMMARY:

KEY POINTS:

- ☐ _____
- ☐ _____
- ☐ _____
- ☐ _____

INCLUDED LINKS:

_____

_____

SHARED ON:

FACEBOOK ☐	INSTAGRAM ☐
TWITTER ☐	PINTEREST ☐
☐	☐

TAGS & KEYWORDS:

_____ ☐

_____ ☐

_____ ☐

# OF COMMENTS:	# OF TRACKBACKS:

NOTES:

Made in the USA
Middletown, DE
25 July 2023

35724886R00068